Bertha Parker

The First Indigenous American
Woman Archaeologist

by Mari Bolte

Image credits: Cover: Smithsonian Institution/Wikimedia; 3: Smithsonian Institution/Wikimedia; 4: Eric Poulin/Shutterstock; 5: Denis Torkhov/Shutterstock; 6: Jeffrey M. Frank/Shutterstock; 8: University of Southern California/Getty Images; 9: paleontologist natural/Shutterstock; 11: Harry Beugelink/Shutterstock; 12: Dominic Gentilcore PhD/Shutterstock; 14: Gorodenkoff/Shutterstock; 15: OlgaMed/Shutterstock; 16: Smithsonian Institution/Wikimedia; 17: Brian Goff/Shutterstock, Pyty/Shutterstock, KASUE/Shutterstock, Piotr Przyluski/Shutterstock, dreibirnen/Shutterstock, Ink Drop/Shutterstock; 19: Kilmer Media/Shutterstock; 20: solkafa/Shutterstock, Vlas Telino studio/Shutterstock, The India Today Group/Getty Images; 21: littlenySTOCK/Shutterstock; 22; Filip Bjorkman/Shutterstock, nadiia_oborska/Shutterstock; 23: Kuryanovich_Viktar/Shutterstock; 24: Michael Ochs Archives/Getty Images; 25: Dika Rio Saputra/Shutterstock; 26: New Africa/Shutterstock; background: incomible/Getty Images

9781223187556 English Hardcover
9781223187563 English Paperback
9781223187570 English eBook

Published by Paw Prints Publishing
PawPrintsPublishing.com
Printed in Canada

See the Glossary on page 29 for definitions of words found in **bold** in the text!

"If you want to see [Bertha's] black eyes shine, talk to her about archaeology, or watch her uncovering something choice."

–Mark Raymond Harrington

Her Kingdom: Archaeology

Gypsum Cave in Nevada is named for the mineral gypsum. Gypsum is formed by ancient seabeds!

The Discovery

It is a hot day at Gypsum Cave, just outside Las Vegas, Nevada. Head **archaeologist** Mark Raymond Harrington is overseeing a dig. His niece, Bertha, has come along to help.

Bertha sees a narrow opening under a slab of rock. She crawls through. The space is tight and dusty. Inside, Bertha makes a discovery. She finds a skull belonging to a giant sloth. The animal **perished** an estimated 10,000 years before Bertha even entered the cave.

Want to learn about other female diggers?! A website called Trowelblazers features notable female archaeologists, paleontologists, and geologists.

Researchers found 17th-century **artifacts** from the Iroquois nations at the Silverheels site, now part of Cattaraugus County, New York.

Born Royal

Bertha Parker was born into **STEAM** royalty in 1907. Her father was Arthur C. Parker, an **Indigenous** archaeologist and historian of the Seneca Nation.

He was working at the Silverheels archaeological site in New York when Bertha was born. Bertha's Seneca name was Yewas. But her family called her "Birdie."

Arthur Parker cofounded a group whose goal was to educate the public about Indigenous people!

Bertha's mother was Beulah Tahamont. She was also Indigenous. An Abenaki actress, she starred in silent films like *Desert Gold* and *The Crimson Challenge*. Beulah and Arthur divorced in 1914, when Bertha was seven years old.

Bertha and Beulah then moved to Los Angeles, California. They tried to build upon Beulah's work and make it in show business. They even toured with the circus! Finally, they got their big break in Western movies, which were starting to become popular.

The "Princess" Lillian St. Cyr

The Native Americans seen in Hollywood Westerns were often played by White actors. But Lillian St. Cyr, a Winnebago woman, brought an Indigenous face onto the silver screen. Going by the stage name Princess Red Wing, she was the first Native American woman to star in a feature film. Her career spanned 15 years. She spoke up for Indigenous people throughout her lifetime.

Archaeologists have to work carefully to remove centuries of dirt from delicate findings.

In the early 1920s, Bertha met and married her first husband, Joseph Pallan. They had one daughter, Wilma Mae. But their marriage was not a happy one and it would not last. Her uncle, Mark Raymond Harrington, also an archaeologist, hired Bertha to help his crew on his digs. Bertha had a natural gift for archaeology, and she began to thrive.

Archaeologists are STEAM-based *scientists* that study the past through unearthed human-made artifacts. They use *technology* to learn more about discovered objects without hurting them. *Engineering* helps them figure out how smaller artifacts might have come from something bigger. Having an *artistic* mind helps them imagine what life might have been like in the past. *Math* is important while on expeditions, too! Bertha mastered all of these areas while helping her uncle. Even without a degree, she became a true "Queen of STEAM."

In Bertha's time, many thought only formally educated people could do that work. It was seen as a "man's job." Her uncle did not agree. Mark trained anyone who was interested. Many of his workers were Indigenous peoples and women. Crew members, like Bertha, were asked to share their ideas. They were given credit in **published** works.

Some archaeologists look for evidence of ancient people and study what their lives were like. For example, a piece of pottery can reveal many things. Where did the clay to make it come from? What did the pot hold? How was it used? Decorations on the outside might show a party scene or a picture of a leader.

Moapa Valley is a desert in Nevada. Animal bones and artifacts are often found in deserts, so archaeologists love to explore there. The dry weather helps keep artifacts preserved.

In 1929, Mark and Bertha studied a pueblo near the Moapa Valley. Bertha called the area Scorpion Hill. The next year, Bertha made a discovery of camel bone **fossils** at a place called Corn Creek near Las Vegas, Nevada. This proved that early humans had lived there. Bertha was skilled at finding things that others missed.

The inside of Gypsum Cave is dry and cool. These conditions have kept ancient animal hair, tissue, and even droppings intact for thousands of years.

A Crown Made of Fossils

In 1930, the dig team moved to Gypsum Cave. They would spend more than a year there. It's where Bertha made her biggest recorded discovery. She found the skull of a giant ground sloth that dated back to 8500 BCE*! The skull was found near ancient human tools. Scientists think that this was the earliest proof of human life in America.

> Gypsum Cave is 300 feet long and 120 feet wide! There are six rooms inside.

*Before Common Era (BCE) is before year 1

Around that time, Bertha met James E. "Thirsty" Thurston. He was a paleontologist. He brought his knowledge of ancient animals to the Gypsum Cave expedition. This would result in the first known dig where paleontologists and archaeologists worked together from beginning to end. He and Bertha fell in love during this time and they married in 1931. Sadly, he died a year later.

Who Are Paleontologists?

Archaeologists study remains to learn more about ancient humans and their culture. Paleontologists study fossils to learn about Earth's nonhuman creatures. Fossils are the remains, or what's left over, of things that were once alive. More than 99 percent of all animals that ever lived are now **extinct**. Paleontologists can tell us what those animals were like.

During her trip to Gypsum Cave, Bertha found more than a skull and a few tools. Inside, there were remains of weapons and **hearths**. Bertha also found pieces of darts and plant **fibers**. She uncovered torches and stone points. And eventually, more of the sloth remains were found. Its claws were 12 inches long!

Archaeologists often uncover signs of ancient human activity, such as stone weapons and tools.

After that, Bertha became a mini celebrity. Her photo was printed on the front pages of newspapers across the country. Readers loved hearing about her findings.

Bertha demonstrated the differences in size of human-made darts found in Gypsum Cave.

A Timeline of Human History

People began migrating out of Africa 60,000 years ago. They spread across the planet. It took around 45,000 years for people to cross Asia, travel across North America, and settle in South America.

200,000 years ago
Humans start in central Africa.

60,000 years ago
Humans move across the Arabian Peninsula.

50,000 years ago
People move across Asia and into Australia.

40,000 years ago
Humans move across Europe. Migration across Asia continues north through Russia.

20,000 years ago
People cross from Russia to Alaska. They move south through Canada and the United States.

15,000 years ago
Humans continue southward through Central and South America.

Sharing the Wealth

Bertha kept making important discoveries. She was supported with grant money and resources for new projects. Her notes and essays were published in many science **journals**. Many of the objects she found were displayed at museums and educational institutions like the Southwest Museum in Los Angeles, California, where Mark worked as a **curator**.

The Southwest Museum was the first museum in Los Angeles. It opened in 1914.

The Southwest Museum is now part of the Autry Museum of the American West. It has been voted "Favorite Museum" by *Los Angeles Daily News* readers every year from 2014 to 2021.

Five "Royal" Museum Facts

1. The word *museum* comes from the word "muse." Muses were inspirational Greek goddesses.

2. The first public museum was built by a Babylonian princess in 530 BCE.

3. The largest and most visited museum in the world is the Louvre in Paris, France. It was first used as a fortress, and then as a royal palace. Today, it's a museum!

4. The oldest museums in the world are the Capitoline Museums in Rome. The collection includes the Capitoline She-Wolf statue, which was once a symbol of the city.

5. The International Museum of Toilets in India has golden toilets that belonged to Roman emperors!

Bertha and her mom drove through southwest Nevada. The area has landscapes of red **sandstone**.

A good "STEAM Queen" looks back at the work they've already done and finds ways to improve. In 1933, Bertha and her mother Beulah took a 700-mile road trip back to the site of one of Bertha's first work trips, Scorpion Hill. Bertha was disappointed. The site had been **looted**. But the trip still inspired her to travel more.

Studying **relics** from the past was a passion for Bertha. But she also loved *speaking with people* as a way to learn about the past. She spent time visiting Indigenous nations across California. She interviewed Paiute, Pomo, Yurok, and Maidu people. Bertha spoke to religious leaders, storytellers, and artists.

Ethnologists like Bertha study people and their ways of life over time.

Bertha, like all scientists, had to do careful research and write well to get her papers published.

Bertha's writings on this time were published in a journal called *Masterkey* that was printed by the Southwest Museum. Readers could follow along on her adventures. They got an up-close view of the people she met. Bertha was fair to those she interviewed. They were named as coauthors in the journal.

Iron Eyes Cody worked in film and TV for his entire career, which lasted over 70 years.

Showbiz Royalty

In 1936, Bertha married her third husband, Espera Oscar de Corti (also known as "Iron Eyes Cody"). Cody was a rising star. He became Hollywood's "go-to" man to play Native American characters. It did not come out until the 1990s that Cody was actually of Italian descent. Many people were shocked and upset to learn of his **misrepresentation**. Many appreciated Cody's quality acting skills, even if he lied. It is unclear if Bertha knew about this because she passed away before the truth came out.

Iron Eyes Cody is most famous for his role in a Keep America Beautiful commercial.

Passing the Crown

The Bertha Parker Cody Award for Native American Women is given to college students studying archaeology or museum studies. It helps them get on-the-job training, education opportunities, and internships. Any Indigenous people from the Americas or Pacific Islands can apply. There is also an Arthur C. Parker Scholarship given in honor of Bertha's father.

Bertha's life story and work continue to inspire archaeologists of all ages.

Bertha spent much of the second half of her life acting in movies and educating the public. She died in 1978 at the age of 71. Her legacy as the first Indigenous female archaeologist lives on. She was a trailblazer, a role model, and a true "queen."

Quiz

1. Bertha explored dig sites primarily in:
   A. Egypt

   B. New Mexico

   C. Nevada

   D. California

2. Archaeologists and paleontologists are different because:
   A. one studies living things and one studies dead things

   B. one studies people and one studies animals

   C. one studies boats and one studies plants

   D. one studies the past and one studies the future

3. Bertha was highly respected as an archaeologist because:
   A. she could find things other people missed

   B. she had famous husbands

   C. she had a PhD

   D. she was skilled at writing poetry

4. Ethnologists like Bertha:
   A. make TV commercials

   B. loot important archaeological sites

   C. decorate pottery with party scenes or pictures of leaders

   D. study people and their ways of life over time

Key: 1) C; 2) B; 3) A; 4) D

Glossary

archaeologist (ar-kee-OL-uh-jist): a scientist who studies bones, tools, and other items from the ancient past

artifacts (AR-tuh-fakts): objects that were made by people in the past

curator (KYUR-ay-tur): a person who is in charge of a particular part of a museum

extinct (ek-STINGKT): no longer existing on Earth

fibers (FAI-berz): thin threads of material

fossils (FAH-sulhz): ancient remains of animals or plants that have been preserved within rock

hearths (HAARTHS): the floors or areas in front of fireplaces

Indigenous (ihn-DI-juh-nuhs): having to do with the peoples who have lived in a particular place for a very long time

journals (JUR-nuhlz): magazines that print information on specific subjects

looted (LOO-tuhd): robbed

misrepresentation (mis-reh-pruh-zen-TAY-shun): to deceive other people about the real way someone or something is

perished (PER-isht): died

published (PUB-lisht): included in a book, magazine, or newspaper

relics (REH-luhks): items from an ancient time, place, or culture

sandstone (SAND-stohn): a type of rock that is formed of many layers built over time

STEAM (STEEM): the fields of Science, Technology, Engineering, Arts, and Mathematics; archaeology is part of science

Survey Your Surroundings

With a caregiver, find an open spot of land. Pretend you are looking for a new place to live. Your goal is to live off the land as much as possible. You may want to grab some tools to help, such as:

- a compass
- string, to mark where you will place your home
- a book on edible plants
- binoculars

Ask yourself the following questions:

- Where does the sun rise and set? Where would you place your front door?
- Are there any edible plants nearby? (Look, don't taste!)
- What kind of animals can you find?
- Do any people already live in the area?
- Are there water sources available?
- What about shade or sun? Will it be easy to stay out of the elements in case of bad weather? Is there enough sun and space to grow food?
- Is your home on a hill? Would you want to build your house at the top of the hill, at the bottom, or somewhere in between? Why?

ACTIVITY

Learn the Land

Everyone in America lives on land that once belonged to a Native Nation. With the help of an adult, visit Native Land Digital at https://native-land.ca.

Find out which Nation has ancestral ties to the place where you live. Learn their history and traditions. What happened to them? Where are those people today? Then, write about that Nation and share with others!

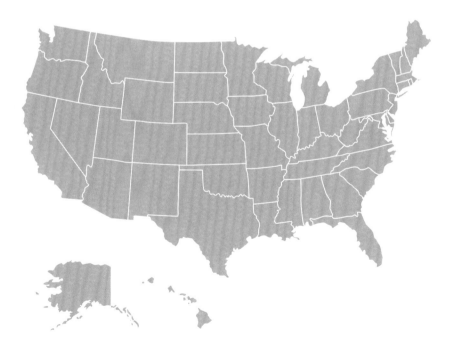

Index

ethnology, 22

giant sloth, 5, 13, 15

Gypsum Cave, 4–5, 12–16

Harrington, Mark Raymond, 5, 9–11, 18

husbands, 9, 14, 25

legacy, 27

Masterkey, 23

paleontology, 5, 14

Pallan, Wilma Mae (daughter), 9

Southwest Museum, 18–19, 23

St. Cyr, Lillian, 8

Tahamont, Beulah, 8, 21